I0027424

Avoiding high-impact conflicts is the factor that makes the difference in terms of business. continuity.

Satisfaction is a positive influence, as much as lack of confidence is a negative one.

Guide to Proper Acting Management in Projects

Creating an environment of trust

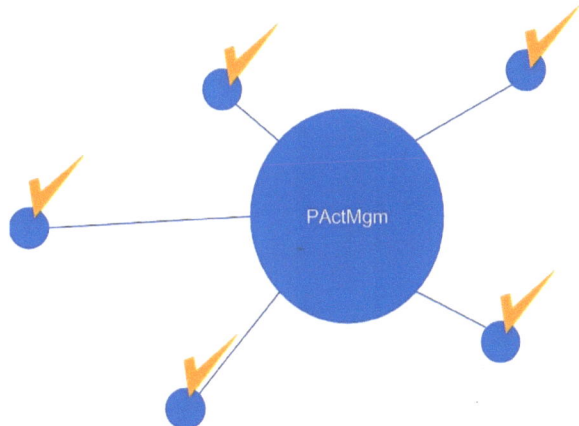

PActMgm

Lic. Alvaro Pochintesta, PMP
alvaro.pochintesta@gmail.com

ISBN: 978-9974-99-934-3

1   Revision History

In order to ensure that you are using the latest version of this document, please subscribe to the original channel where you acquired it and keep yourself up to date.

Date	Version	Description	Author
Nov. 26, 2014	1.0	First version published	Alvaro Pochintesta
Jan. 14, 2015	1.1	Corrections due to revisions and contributions	Alvaro Pochintesta
Jan. 26, 2015	1.2	Corrections due to revisions and contributions	Alvaro Pochintesta
Jun. 29, 2015	1.3	Translation to English	Alvaro Pochintesta
Jul. 06, 2015	1.4	Information included: Copyright and ISBN	Alvaro Pochintesta

2   Contents

3   Preface

First of all, I would like to thank you for downloading and reading this guide, which I wrote with the hope that it will be really useful.

I have been working for many years in this field and hope to have achieved a methodology that is both clear and easy to follow.

I will greatly appreciate every comment, criticism or contribution sent to alvaro.pochintesta@gmail.com

This guide is intended to be applied on projects managed according to PMI™ (www.pmi.org) guidelines, as defined in the PMBOK™ (Project Management Body Of Knowledge).

For those who have the responsibilities specified in this guide, or any Project Manager role, it is strongly recommended to follow the PMI™ Code of Ethics

Using this guide without paying the corresponding royalties is in itself an example of non-proper acting.

4   Prologue

Some years ago, when I spoke about Project Management, I often had to explain what it was about, as if it were necessary to demonstrate its importance. Nowadays, a successful project is only conceivable with a formal management, done by a professional Project Manager.

There are, therefore, two important questions:

1   Is it admissible that Risk Management be ignored in a project?

2   How important is stakeholders' Proper Acting?

State of the art in Project Management leaves no doubt about the answer to the first question. The same applies to Management of Time, Cost, Quality, Scope, Communications, Human Resources or any other knowledge areas.

But, regarding my second question...

We already know the consequences of leaving Risk Management unattended.

And what about leaving Proper Acting unattended?
Are we not aware of the consequences?

Please ask yourself this question:

Is Proper Acting not managed because it is not important, or because we lack the right tools?

Or even worse: because of lack of interest.

Consequences of skipping Proper Acting Management are as important as those of skipping Risk Management practices.

This document is a guide to Proper Acting Management in projects.

How?

As there appears to exist little or no literature regarding Proper Acting Management, it may seem that there are currently no adequate tools. The same may seem to anyone who is not familiar with Risk Management tools.

Risks! – How to manage something of that sort?

Those tools exist: it is just that we are not used to regarding them as useful for these management needs.

Just as we can define what a risk is, or what the scope of a project is, we can also define what a malicious act is.

We will see how its management involves needs, communication, goals, risks, expectations, strengths, opportunities, weaknesses and threats, among other concepts.

We already have the tools to manage all these aspects.

5 Introduction

When we speak about Proper Acting, this concept is implicitly related to intention. Proper Acting implies that there is no bad intention.

Along this guide:

A malicious act is one performed being aware that it will have negative consequences.

"Being aware" means that one knows what the result may be; but it is also a malicious act when one does not verify the information as it should be.

Proper Acting not only implies being conscious of not causing negative consequences to someone else, but we also need to base ourselves in reliable information to ensure that.

Proper Acting is achieved by everyone involved "before acting", "while acting" and "after acting".

We must be responsible for acting properly, communicating the necessary information so that everyone is conscious of the consequences of their actions, and of reporting possible malicious acts.

When a malicious act occurs, we must ensure that the damage is compensated, and that future similar actions are avoided in the future.

Proper Acting generates trust: but good communication is essential for this to happen.

It comes as a result of intention, prudence and responsibility.

6   Goals

The goals of this guide are:

1. To provide a methodological guide to minimize the probability of malicious acts based upon *awareness*;

2. To validate every *intention* before it ends up in a malicious act;

3. To verify every possible *action* in order to detect these acts in a timely manner when they do occur;

4. To provide the elements for managing the compensation of every *damage* caused;

5. To provide a methodological guide aligned with PMI (Project Management Institute).

6. To provide a methodological guide aligned with PDCA[1] model, so that:

- ● Plan: Awareness   - Plan to avoid malicious acts.
- ● Do: Intention   - Validate all intentions.
- ● Check: Action   - Verify actions.
- ● Act: Damage   - Compensate every damage and avoid similar actions in the future.

---

[1] PDCA (Plan, Do, Check, Act) - https://en.wikipedia.org/wiki/PDCA

7   Benefits

7.1   Builds Credibility

Credibility comes as a result of regular reporting about Proper Acting Management performance, following a formal methodology.

7.2   Eases Conflict Resolution

Provides tools to prove or discard malicious acts that may arise conflicts.

7.3   Eases Negotiation

Supplies a true environment of trust, suitable to negotiate options and reach agreements.

7.4   Improves Communication and Relationship

Generates communications that prove Proper Acting, which improves relationships.

7.5   Creates a "Good Experience" (Satisfaction)

In an environment where there is a permanent perception of Proper Acting, a sense of satisfaction is easily achieved.

7.6   Generates Relationships of Trust and Continuity

When relationships based on trust are achieved, their continuity is a natural result.

8   Definitions

Here follows a non-exhaustive list of definitions of some terms used in this guide.

Please do not skip reading the following definitions:

Act	To do something for a particular purpose or to solve a problem. http://dictionary.cambridge.org/es/diccionario/britanico/act
Avoid	1. Prevent from happening. http://www.oxforddictionaries.com/definition/english/avoid 2. For our purposes, in order to align with PMI's Guide, we will understand it as: "To eliminate the threat of a negative risk".
Awareness	Knowledge that something exists, or understanding of a situation or subject at the present time based on information or experience. http://dictionary.cambridge.org/es/diccionario/britanico/awareness
Consequence	A result or effect, typically one that is unwelcome or unpleasant.

	http://www.oxforddictionaries.com/definition/english/consequence
Compensate	Give (someone) something, typically money, in recognition of loss, suffering, or injury incurred; recompense. http://www.oxforddictionaries.com/definition/english/compensate
Damage	Detrimental effects. http://www.oxforddictionaries.com/definition/english/damage
Expectation	A strong belief that something will happen or be the case. http://www.oxforddictionaries.com/definition/english/expectation
Intention	Something that you want and plan to do. http://dictionary.cambridge.org/es/diccionario/britanico/intention
Malicious	Intended to harm or upset other people. http://dictionary.cambridge.org/es/diccionario/britanico/malicious
Necessary	Determined, existing, or happening by natural laws or predestination; inevitable.

	http://www.oxforddictionaries.com/definition/english/necessary
Opportunity	A time or set of circumstances that makes it possible to do something. http://www.oxforddictionaries.com/definition/english/opportunity
Prudencia	The quality of being prudent; cautiousness. http://www.oxforddictionaries.com/definition/english/prudence
Proper	Of the required or correct type or form; suitable or appropriate. http://www.oxforddictionaries.com/definition/english/proper
Responsibility	1. To have a duty to work for or help someone who is in a position of authority over you. 2. Blame for something that has happened. 3. Good judgment and the ability to act correctly and make decisions on your own. http://dictionary.cambridge.org/es/diccionario/britanico/responsibility
Risk	1. Something bad that might happen.

	http://dictionary.cambridge.org/es/diccionario/britanico/risk 2 - As defined by PMI: "Project risk is an uncertain event or condition that, if it occurs, has a positive or negative effect on one or more project objectives such as scope, schedule, cost, and quality."
Will	The mental power used to control and direct your thoughts and actions, or a determination to do something, despite any difficulties or opposition. http://dictionary.cambridge.org/es/diccionario/britanico/will

9   Proper Acting Management Policy

Proper Acting is managed by "avoiding" malicious acts, from a positive perspective, easing communication and sharing necessary information in an atmosphere of friendly relations.

Every person involved in the project must be informed that Proper Acting is being managed, as well as the methodology that is being used.

Each stakeholder is responsible for his own Proper Acting and everyone else's, persuading and reporting if he knows or suspects about bad intentions.

Proper Acting should generate confidence in a friendly and relaxed atmosphere. If a conflict arises, bad intention should be discarded if no proof is found.

Achieving Proper Acting must be a goal. There should be a clear definition of the necessary actions to reach it, responsibilities, how to measure and factors that determine its success.

10 Guidelines

In order to achieve the maximum transparency, Proper Acting Management must be conducted by a (natural or legal) person external to the project and with no personal interest in it. He must interact fluently with every stakeholder.

The person in charge of Proper Acting Management must not have any other role in the project, nor any rapport with any person involved.

The Project Manager must act like a facilitator in this management, providing:

- Necessary resources (financial, human, time, infrastructure).
- Coordination between involved organizations.
- Inclusion in the activities of the project, meetings and other instances where he might be required.
- Support in management (with every stakeholder, especially for getting and ensuring their support).
- Access to all required information.
- Alignment of Proper Acting Management methodology with the management methodology of the project.
- Collaboration in specific work instances of Proper Acting Management.
- In particular, management of stakeholders and communications must be approved by the Proper Acting Manager; he must therefore facilitate all approval cycles.

The Proper Acting Manager must provide the following information to the Project Manager:

- Dependencies required from him and from the project for Proper Acting managing, indicating the necessary resources.
- Recommendations for avoiding actions that could be misinterpreted (potential conflicts).

- Identifying potential malicious acts.
- Recommendations for compensating damages consequential of malicious acts.
- Recommendations for preventing future occurrences of malicious acts.

The Proper Acting Manager has the following responsibilities:
- MANAGING TO **AVOID** THE OCCURRENCE OF MALICIOUS ACTS.
- Determining if an act should be considered malicious when there is no consensus between the parties (conflict of interests) – This is potentially the most controversial responsibility and the one that requires more support from the start.
- Ensuring compliance with the goals of Proper Acting Management.
- Providing periodical feedback on his own management performance.
- Interacting in a prudent, respectful and friendly way without interfering with the performance of the project.
- Escalating immediately every situation that involves risks through the appropriate channels as defined in the Communications Plan.
- Maintain confidentiality, reserve and discretion corresponding to the defined levels.
- Strictly stick to ethics (it is recommended to base upon PMI Code of Ethics, as mentioned at the beginning of this guide).

11   Methodology

11.1 Base Concepts

Before introducing the formal methodology and its corresponding processes, let us mention the concepts on which it is based:

For there to be a malicious act, there must be *intent* and this implies that there is *awareness*.

Awareness implies knowledge, which in turn implies *information*.

If there is *awareness* (information) of other people's needs, then we consider that there exists *intention* in an *action* that causes a *damage*.

Let us emphasize the following four concepts:

- **Awareness** for having information of the others' needs;
- **Intention** because, being aware, there is a decision to act;
- **Action** because there has to exist a real act;
- **Damage** because there has to exist a damage arising from the action.

Therefore, action must be taken on these four concepts:

- Ensure Awareness

  Because if there is Awareness (there must exist a *record* stating that the *information* about stakeholders' *needs, interests* and *expectations* was *communicated*), then *intention* cannot be denied, so there exists a *responsibility* of *compensating* the *damage* caused.

- Validate[2] Intention

  There is always the possibility of misunderstanding or miscommunication, so it is imperative that intentions are clearly validated against expectations.

- Verify[3] Action

  Likewise, actions may occur that cause damage. The key point is to *identify in time* when they occur and to determine if they were intentional. Because of this, it is mandatory to verify that those actions have caused no damage.

- Compensate Damage

  Finally, it is essential that if there are damages due to malicious acts, they are compensated. Otherwise the management fails (the reason is usually because of lack of support and commitment, which must be obtained in the startup phase).

---

[2] Validate: In this guide, validating means ensuring that what was done (or is going to be done) is really what was (or is) intended to be done.

[3] Verify: For the purposes of this guide, to verify means ensuring that what was done was what had been agreed (what should have been done).

11.2 The Four Pillars of Proper Acting Management

As a result of what we just said, having identified four fundamental concepts in which we must focus, and having defined the framework of actions that must be taken respect each one, let us define the following **Four Pillars of Proper Acting:**

Ensure Awareness

Ensure that there exists Awareness through the *Needs Information Knowledge Formal Record* by means of Communications Management.

Validate Intention

Ensure Communication and Record of the Information on *Intentions validated against the Stakeholders' Expectations*.

Verify Action

Permanent evaluation of the *Consequences of Acts verifying if there exists Damage* caused by bad intention.

Compensate Damage

If there exists damage caused by a malicious act, the *injured must be compensated*. This concept includes taking action in order to avoid future occurrences.

11.3 Proper Acting Management Success

Proper Acting Management:

- Is Successful   - when there are no malicious acts.
- Is Valid   - when every damage is compensated.
- Fails   - when some damage is not compensated.

11.4 Example

Let us now see an example that introduces also other concepts (known in management environments):

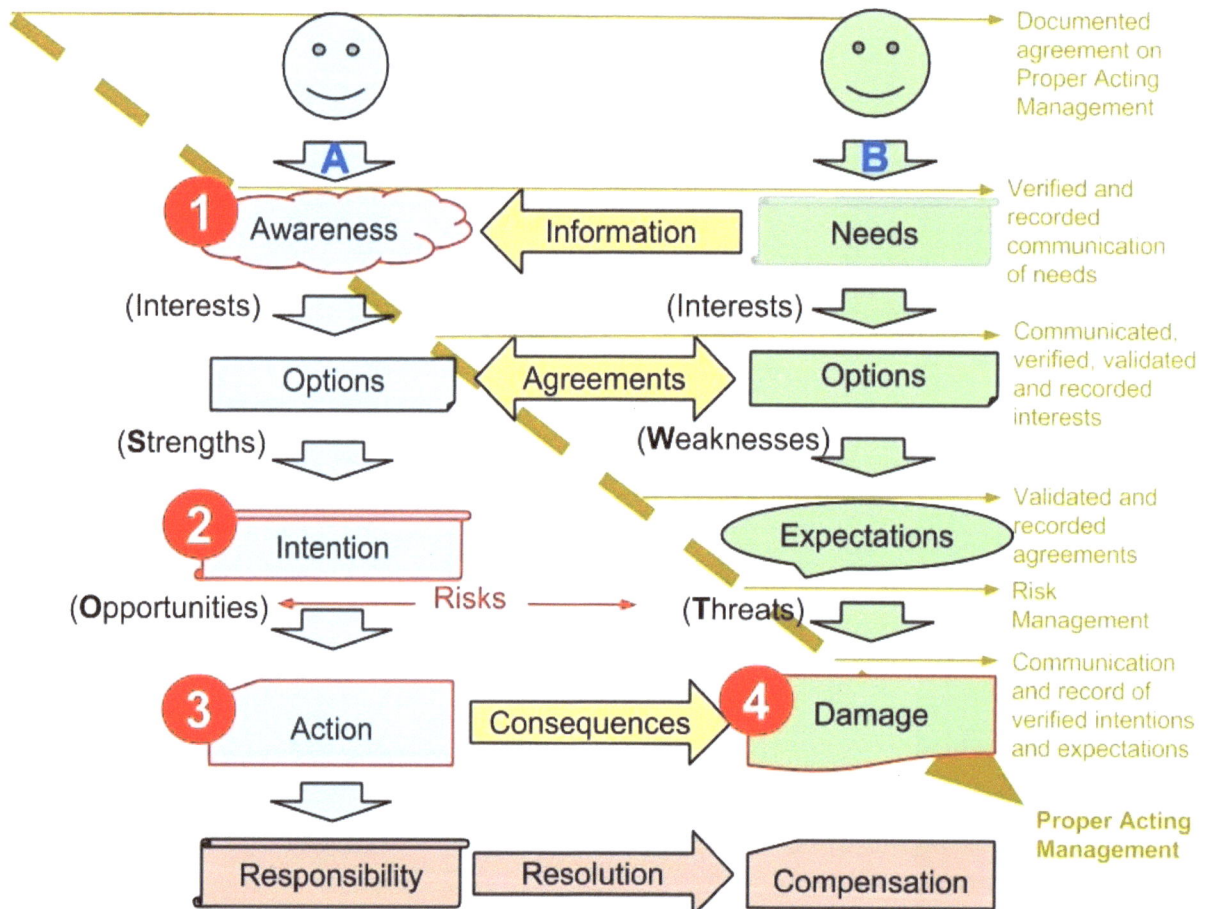

We can see a brown arrow crossing diagonally, which represents Proper Acting Management. In each instance, another horizontal arrow of the same color springs from the main one, pointing to actions that correspond to Proper Acting Management in that instance.

➢ If "A" knows the needs of "B", then he has information on them and is therefore aware of them.

➢ Both parties have interests: "A" has them with awareness of the needs of "B", while "B" has them based on his own needs.

➢ Both of them have options, upon which agreements are reached.

➢ Later, in the context of the execution of the agreements, "A" may have certain Strengths and "B" certain Weaknesses.

➢ Based on this, "A" (being aware) may have certain intention and "B" certain expectations on that matter.

➢ In a context of risks, this means that "A" may exploit opportunities that pose threats to "B".

➢ Having the opportunity, "A" executes an action that causes damage to "B".

➢ Finally, the resolution of the conflict on the action that caused damage should be done by means of a compensation paid by "A".

Resuming this example, we will focus on Awareness, Intention, Action and Damage, always taking into account that:

- There is intention when there is awareness.
- There is awareness when there is information.
- An act is malicious if it is performed with intention and it causes damage.

11.5 Synthesis

Based upon what was explained above, we propose the methodology for Proper Acting Management, focusing on four aspects (Pillars) and defining the action framework on them:

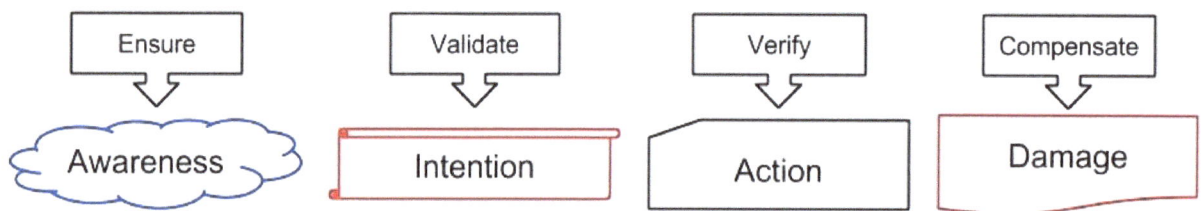

Ensure	Validate	Verify	Compensate
Awareness	Intention	Action	Damage

Remember these four points:

1. Ensure Awareness
2. Validate Intention
3. Verify Action
4. Compensate Damage

Easy to remember:

1. Awareness is what determines intention: we must Ensure it exists.

2. Intention might be misinterpreted: we must Validate it was properly understood.

3. Action may cause damage: we must Verify it occurred.

4. Finally, Damage must be Compensated.

12   Processes

This proposed methodology for Proper Acting Management in projects is organized in process guidelines: input elements, tools and techniques, and output elements. In turn, in order to align this methodology with the guide of the PMI, processes are grouped following the same criteria: Initiating, Planning, Executing, Monitoring and Controlling, and Closing groups.

In turn, processes can be implemented to the level of intensity that is considered appropriate for each project. In this guide, three levels are offered:

Level 1	<u>**Present**</u>	**- Minimal Proper Acting Management, but it is *present* in the project**
		Best practices and guidelines are followed, but no formal processes are implemented, nor there exists strong support for this management.
		>>FOR TRUSTED ENVIRONMENTS - This level is only suitable for projects with no more than 3 stakeholders, with a certain level of trust among them; the only goal is to prevent "misunderstandings" or "misinterpreted acts" in order to avoid conflicts.
Level 2	<u>**Formal**</u>	**- Processes defined in the methodology are implemented and followed**
		Proper Acting Management is performed by a person assigned for this role, who is responsible for the implementation of the processes defined in the methodology. There exists strong support for this management.

		NORMAL USE OF THE METHODOLOGY - This is the appropriate level to "Build a legitimate environment of trust", because Proper Acting Management is formally managed, and this management has the adequate support.
Level 3	**Strong**	**- Proper Acting Management is applied with a high level of rigurosity** *This level should be implemented in environments where the existence of negative precedents or previous bad experiences among the stakeholders cause a bad disposition or the risk of imminent conflicts.* **>>FOR CONFLICTUAL ENVIRONMENTS -** In this case, applying the methodology at its strongest level will avoid conflicts and may even heal the relationship if there exists good intention among the stakeholders.

NOTE! **Colors identify each level as follows:**

1. >>Present - **Orange** (Starts with "**>>**")
2. Formal **- Black**
3. >>Strong **- Blue** (Starts with "**>>**")

NOTE! **References to Technical Elements are in CAPITAL LETTERS**

References to technical elements, whether documents or concepts used in project management, are written in CAPITAL LETTERS. Readers not familiar with this subject may find almost all of them in the PMI's Guide (PMBOK) mentioned earlier in this document.

The following table shows the organization of the processes in the five groups:

Initiating Process Group
P01: Obtaining support for the management P02: Communicating that Proper Acting will be managed
Planning Process Group
P03: Planning Awareness Assurance P04: Planning Intentions Validation P05: Planning Actions Verification P06: Planning Damage Compensation
Executing Process Group
P07: Ensuring Awareness P08: Validating Intention P09: Compensating Damage
Monitoring and Controlling Process Group
P10: Verifying Action P11: Reporting management performance
Closing Process Group
P12: Sharing best practices and lessons learned P13: Registering the management level of success P14: Closing contracts

12.1 Initiating Processes

In the initiating processes we must be aware that agreements that are not achieved in the first stages are very hard to achieve later and frequently end up arising conflicts.

12.1.1 Process – P01: Obtaining Support for the Management

The goal of this process is to:

>>Agree that guidelines and best practices of Proper Acting will be followed.

Ensure support to Proper Acting Management in the highest (hierarchical) levels. This means that resources will be supplied and management actions will be backed.

>>Stakeholders must sign a professionally advised contract, committing to compensate every damage caused, as determined by the Proper Acting Manager.

12.1.1.1 P01 – Input Elements

- STAKEHOLDER REGISTER

12.1.1.2 P01 – Tools and Techniques

- Make a presentation to the SPONSOR and representatives of the parties involved with power of decision, in order to explain the benefits of Proper Acting Management in the project.
- Share best practices and lessons learned in other projects respect to this matter, that may apply to this one.

12.1.1.3   P01 – Output Elements

- Meeting minute with the agreement stating that Proper Acting will be managed in the project and that it will be backed by the sponsor and the stakeholders.
- Clause in the PROJECT CHARTER stating that Proper Acting will be managed, backed by the sponsor and the stakeholders. The methodology that will be used must be described.
- >>Contract signed by stakeholders committing to compensate the damage caused.

12.1.2   Process – P02: Communicating that Proper Acting will be managed

The goal of this process is to commit every stakeholder with Proper Acting Management, so that they *understand their responsibilities* on the four pillars involved, mainly from a perspective of "avoiding", where they are expected to *communicate needs, interests and expectations to ensure Awareness.*

>> Communicate that a Proper Acting Management methodology will be applied, that it is backed by a contract among the parts, and that its management will be strict, with the consequences that it may imply.

12.1.2.1   P02 – Input Elements

- PROJECT CHARTER

12.1.2.2   P02 – Tools and Techniques

Use the KICK OFF stage to communicate the stakeholders the following:

- That Proper Acting will be managed in this project
- What Proper Acting means
- The Proper Acting Management policy
- The backup this management has in this project
- The methodology to be used
- Who this management involves
- Who the managers are
- The four Proper Acting Management pillars
- The goals
- The agreement to compensate damage caused by bad intention

12.1.2.3   P02 – Output Elements

- Record in the meeting minute about all subjects related to Proper Acting Management that were discussed.
- >> The meeting minute must be signed by the stakeholders.

12.2 Planning Processes

>> Plan instances for reviewing Best Practices and agreements related to Proper Acting.

Planning processes are meant to ensure that the four Pillars of Proper Acting Management will be managed through the different Project Management Knowledge Areas involved.

The four pillars will be managed in the following Knowledge Areas:

Proper Acting Management Pillar	Project Management Knowledge Areas
Ensure Awareness	Stakeholder Management
	Communications Management
Intention Validation	Communications Management
	Risk Management
Verify Action	Risk Management
Compensate Damage	Risk Management

12.2.1   Process – P03: Planning Awareness Assurance

>> Planning the information that must be shared among stakeholders to Ensure Awareness and the way it will be communicated.

One of the four pillars of Proper Acting Management is to "Ensure Awareness". This means that every stakeholder is aware of the needs, interests and expectations of the others, in order to make clear the responsibility for their actions when they cause damage (of which they were aware because there exists recorded evidence that the information was communicated). This assigns responsibility and therefore the commitment to compensate.

>> Plan the way in which Awareness Assurance will be managed, being pessimistic and considering that bad intention will exist (high probability in Risk Management terms).

12.2.1.1   P03 – Input Elements

- STAKEHOLDER REGISTER
- STAKEHOLDER MANAGEMENT PLAN
- PROJECT CHARTER
- PROJECT SCOPE STATEMENT
- COMMUNICATIONS MANAGEMENT PLAN

12.2.1.2   P03 – Tools and Techniques

- We must ensure the following for each stakeholder:
  1. That his needs, interests and expectations will be formally documented throughout the whole project.
  2. That he will be informed about the needs, interests and expectations of the other stakeholders.
- Plan concrete instances of Communication in the COMMUNICATIONS MANAGEMENT PLAN to ensure the two points mentioned above.
- >> Stakeholders must:
  1. Sign a document stating that all their needs, interests and expectations are the ones they communicated.

2. Sign a document each time they receive this information about other stakeholder.

12.2.1.3   P03 – Output Elements

- COMMUNICATIONS MANAGEMENT PLAN - Updated
- Intentions Register (Register of Intentions, Interests, Needs and Expectations of all the stakeholders)
- RISK MANAGEMENT PLAN - Updated

12.2.2   Process – P04: Planning Intentions Validation

>> Dialog instances must be planned for permanently validating intentions.

The goal of this process is to plan to ensure that the intentions of every stakeholder will be validated against the others' expectations, which must be aligned with their needs and interests. This validation must be performed before executing each action.

>> Each stakeholder must be formally committed to declare his intentions, for them to be validated before each action (any event related to the project); if he fails to do so, it will be implicitly interpreted as a malicious act.

12.2.2.1   P04 – Input Elements

- Intentions Register
- STAKEHOLDER REGISTER
- STAKEHOLDER MANAGEMENT PLAN
- COMMUNICATIONS MANAGEMENT PLAN

12.2.2.2   P04 – Tools and Techniques

- Worksheet that implements a matrix matching in separate sheets each stakeholder's actions validated against the others' expectations.
- Plan dialog instances for validating intentions before executing actions.

12.2.2.3   P04 – Output Elements

- Intentions Register - Updated
- STAKEHOLDER REGISTER - Updated
- STAKEHOLDER MANAGEMENT PLAN - Updated
- COMMUNICATIONS MANAGEMENT PLAN - Updated
- >> Statement signed by all stakeholders committing themselves to inform their intentions before each action, assuming the responsibility that, when failing to do so, the action will be considered malicious.

12.2.3   Process – P05: Planning Actions Verification

>> Instances must be planned to verify that the actions have caused no damage.

The goal of this process is to plan how to perform the verification that the executed actions have caused no intentional damage.

>> It should be planned so that, when actions occur, it is verified **as soon as possible** whether they caused harm to others; for this, mechanisms must be implemented to quickly detect an action when it was not planned.

12.2.3.1   P05 – Input Elements

- Refer to any project document that records actions (events related to this project)
- Intentions Register

12.2.3.2   P05 – Tools and Techniques

- It is convenient to identify Actions that imply negative risks which may eventually harm others; for this, we may refer to the Project Management Plan and other Related Documents.
- Implement an Action Register, each of which may have a reference to a project event:
    - A Task in the elaboration of a product
    - A Communication
    - A Review / Verification / Validation of a Deliverable
    - Etc.

12.2.3.3   P05 – Output Elements

- Project Documentation - Updated
- Intentions Register - Updated

12.2.4   Process – P06: Planning Damage Compensation

>> Agree the commitment to compensate when there exists damage arising from an action that may be interpreted as malicious.

The goal of this process is to plan how to compensate damage arising from malicious acts.

>> In an extreme level, it is recommended that stakeholders make a deposit in guarantee of possible damages they may cause. This should be supported by an explicit authorization (signed document) to invoke the guarantee by the responsible of Proper Acting Management.

12.2.4.1 P06 – Input Elements

- PROJECT CHARTER
- STAKEHOLDER REGISTER
- Involved CONTRACTS

12.2.4.2 P06 – Tools and Techniques

At this time it is very difficult to reach agreements not made in the initial stages. The best tool to plan damage compensation is to reach previous agreements:

- Document Agreements on damage compensation.
- Ensure support to Proper Acting Management as mentioned in the processes of the Initiating Group.
- Strictly apply Risk Management methodologies. Include potential damage in Project Risk Management.

12.2.4.3 P06 – Output Elements

- PROJECT MANAGEMENT PLAN - Updated
- CONTRACTS - Updated
- RISK MANAGEMENT PLAN - Updated

12.3 Executing Processes

12.3.1 Process – P07: Ensuring Awareness

>> Run as scheduled the instances to share information about expectations, needs and interests.

The goal of this process is to run the actions planned to ensure awareness through formal communication of stakeholders' expectations, needs and interests.

>> Non-cooperation, not providing information or not acknowledging receipt of it, will mean itself a malicious act.

12.3.1.1 P07 – Input Elements

- COMMUNICATIONS PLAN
- STAKEHOLDER REGISTER
- Intentions Register

12.3.1.2 P07 – Tools and Techniques

- Communicate expectations, needs and interests as defined in the plan.
- Formally record communications; *these will be the evidence of bad intention* if it should occur.

12.3.1.3 P07 – Output Elements

- Communications register

12.3.2   Process – P08: Validating Intention

>> Before each action, validate that the intention does not undermine expectations, needs or interests of other stakeholders.

The goal of this process is to validate, before their execution, that actions correspond to intentions and do not undermine stakeholders' expectations.

>> Level 3 implies that at this point, each stakeholder must ask for the approval of the Proper Acting Manager to execute each action.

12.3.2.1   P08 – Input Elements

- Intentions Register

12.3.2.2   P08 – Tools and Techniques

- For planned actions, validate that their intentions match the Intentions Register.
- For non planned actions, communicate intentions to all the stakeholders and validate them against every stakeholders' expectations, needs and interests.

12.3.2.3   P08 – Output Elements

- Intentions Register - Updated (approval to execute the related action must be recorded).

12.3.3   Process – P09: Compensate Damage

>> Damage must be compensated according to the previous agreements.

The goal of this process is that damage is compensated, and that a plan is defined and executed as soon as possible to avoid future occurrences of similar situations.

>> We should be very strict with the execution of all possible actions to compensate the damage caused and prevent future recurrence, even if it means applying penalty clauses in contracts, invoking guarantee deposits, etc.

12.3.3.1   P09 – Input Elements

- Contracts
- Intentions Register

12.3.3.2   P09 – Tools and Techniques

- Ask for legal advice from a professional.
- Use Negotiation and Conflict Resolution methodologies.

12.3.3.3   P09 – Output Elements

- Project Documentation - Updated (impact all involved documentation under the new scenario).
- Contracts - Updated.
- Record of Satisfaction with the performed compensation to the victims.

- Actions for Avoiding future similar events, impacted on the Project Management Plan.

12.4 Monitoring and Controlling Processes

12.4.1 Process – P10: Verifying Action

>> Upon the implementation of an action, we must obtain consensus of stakeholders that it caused no harm.

The goal of this process is, once an action is implemented, whether planned or not, (detected late or in time), to verify that it caused no harm to stakeholders.

>> Upon implementation of planned actions, we must verify and formally record the compliance by all stakeholders of having suffered no injury. Upon execution of unplanned actions, they will be considered malicious by default, which may be reversed with the approval of all stakeholders. Damage caused by unplanned actions exists in itself for having caused uncertainty in planning and will be subject to responsibility on any consequential damage (*Residual Risks* to be more specific in terms of Management).

12.4.1.1 P10 – Input Elements

- Intentions Register
- STAKEHOLDER REGISTER
- RISK MANAGEMENT PLAN
- PROJECT MANAGEMENT PLAN
- Other involved Project Documentation

12.4.1.2   P10 – Tools and Techniques

- Use TRACEABILITY MATRIXES to detect potential impacts between involved factors.

12.4.1.3   P10 – Output Elements

- Documented agreement on that the action caused no harm (in case it did not).
- Documentation proving that the action caused damage, and actions to trigger the compensation process (in case it did).
- Project Documentation - Updated

12.4.2   Process – P11: Reporting Management Performance

>> Communicate actions and instances where Proper Acting guidelines and best practices have been applied.

The goal of this process is to build trust and credibility through permanent information and transparency.

>> Stakeholders must acknowledge receipt (formally) of these reports; failure to do so will be considered in itself a malicious act. This way, there will be a record of their knowledge about the activities of this management.

12.4.2.1   P11 – Input Elements

- Project Documents (mainly STATUS REPORTS and MEETING MINUTES).

- Record of performed actions and occurred events related to Proper Acting Management.
- RISK REGISTER
- Intentions Register

12.4.2.2   P11 – Tools and Techniques

- Performance Reports including:
    - Reported lapse
    - Actions in the lapse and their status
    - Actions scheduled for the next lapse to be reported
    - Required dependencies
    - Identified risks (related to Proper Acting Management)
    - Occurred risks (related to Proper Acting Management)
    - Controversies
    - Comments
    - Feedback
- Send Reports through the communication channels defined in the Communications Management Plan

12.4.2.3   P11 – Output Elements

- Proper Acting Management Performance Report

12.5 Closing Processes

12.5.1 Process – P12: Sharing best practices and lessons learned

>> There must be an instance for sharing best practices and lessons learned so that they become a contribution for future projects.

The goal of this process is to contribute to a knowledge base focused on improving.

>> It is expected that, in the absence of malicious acts, this instance contributes to settlement if there were negative predispositions.

12.5.1.1 P12 – Input Elements

- Best Practices and Lessons Learned Register

12.5.1.2 P12 – Tools and Techniques

- Hold a session for sharing best practices and lessons learned.

12.5.1.3 P12 – Output Elements

- Meeting minute
- Best Practices and Lessons Learned Register - Updated

12.5.2   Process – P13: Record the management success level

>> There must be an instance to communicate the success level reached on Proper Acting Management.

The goal of this process is to record the success level reached on Proper Acting Management and the consensus of the stakeholders on it.

>> The stakeholders' agreement on the achieved success level will denote transparency in management.

12.5.2.1   P13 – Input Elements

- Intentions Register
- Project Documentation

12.5.2.2   P13 – Tools and Techniques

- Prepare a report with the results achieved in Proper Acting Management and distribute it among stakeholders.

12.5.2.3   P13 – Output Elements

- Report on the success level reached in Proper Acting Management.

12.5.3 Process – P14: Closing contracts

>> Close agreements or contracts related to Proper Acting Management.

The goal of this process is to formally close the contracts that governed the Proper Acting Management.

>> The closure of these contracts implies the end of their effects within the scope of the project. They may continue outside its scope if there are any pending actions.

12.5.3.1 P14 – Input Elements

- Contracts

12.5.3.2 P14 – Tools and Techniques

- Project Documents and other documents that prove the conclusion of stages or agreements.

12.5.3.3 P14 – Output Elements

- Closed Contracts

13 Responsibility

The use of this document or any concept presented in it, does not imply any liability for its author. The author is not liable for damages arising from the implementation of this guide or any part thereof.

14 Intellectual Property

14.1 General Framework

A person shall be entitled to a patent unless --

(a)   the invention was known or used by others in this country, or patented or described in a printed publication in this or a foreign country, before the invention thereof by the applicant for patent, or

…"

(a) "Printed publication"

23.   35 U.S.C. Section 102(a) and (b) states that a "printed publication" constitutes prior art. In a general sense, a reference is proven to be a "printed publication" upon a satisfactory showing that such document has been disseminated or otherwise made available to the extent that persons interested and ordinarily skilled in the subject matter or art, exercising reasonable diligence, can locate it.[8]

24.   MPEP §2128 confirms that an electronic publication, including an online database or Internet publication, is considered to be a "printed publication" within the meaning of 35 U.S.C. 102(a) and (b), provided the publication was accessible to persons concerned with the art to which the document relates. Indeed, in *In re Wyer*, the court stated: "Accordingly, whether information is printed, handwritten, or on microfilm or a magnetic disc or tape, etc., the one who wishes to characterize the information, in whatever form it may be, as a 'printed publication' *** should produce sufficient proof of its dissemination or that it has otherwise been available and accessible to persons concerned with the art to which the document relates and thus most likely to avail themselves of its contents" (citation omitted).[9]

Source: http://www.wipo.int/edocs/mdocs/scp/en/scp_4/scp_4_5.pdf

This guide is registered in Proof of Existence: http://www.proofofexistence.com/

14.2 Explicit Authorization of Use

Use of this guide is authorized in the following cases:

1. The author has given his written consent for its use in a non-profit project that benefits other people.
2. It was obtained by a paid download, which entitles the downloader to use it in for-profit projects.

The payment mechanism is accessible on the same website this guide is published.

The payment transaction receipt is considered sufficient proof of actual pay.

15 Acknowledgements

I want to express my acknowledgement to my mother, with whom I began speaking of the idea before writing anything; friends and colleagues who have collaborated revising this guide. They have contributed with valuable opinions that showed genuine interest, goodwill, professionalism and a lot of attention. No words may thank the time and dedication they gave me.

Mercedes Hernández
(My motivation to develop the idea)

Leonel More, CSM, PMP, ITIL
(Reviewer)

A/S Pablo Etchandy
(The most committed throughout the process) - Thanks my friend Pablo

Dr. Diego Julien López
(Legal advice)

Carlos Pochintesta
(Reviewer)

www.ingramcontent.com/pod-product-compliance
Lightning Source LLC
Chambersburg PA
CBHW060810270326
41928CB00002B/43